The Voice of Amhaj

TRIGUEIRINHO

The Voice of Amhaj

Editorial Revision by

Artur de Paula Carvalho

The profits generated from sales of books by Trigueirinho and his associates will be used to support the non-profit activities of the Shasti Association to disseminate their work.

Original Title in Portuguese:
A VOZ DE AMHAJ

Cover photograph: Clovis Loureiro

Translation and revision: John David Cutrell and Yatri (Frances O'Gorman, Ph. D.)

Cataloging-in-Publication data

Trigueririnho Netto, José
The Voice of Amhaj
Trigueirinho. – Mount Shasta, CA, Shasti Association 2rd edition, 2021
120 p.
ISBN: 978-1-948430-07-4
Library of Congress Control Number: 2021930528

1. Spirituality
2. Ascended Masters
3. New Age
I. Title.

Shasti Association
P.O. Box 318
Mt. Shasta, CA 96067-0318
editorial@shasti.org
www.shasti.org

I have been waiting for this moment to contact you. Humanity very easily slows its steps, forgetting its higher destiny. But the time has come. My Voice must resonate and bring together those who belong to this Ray. I ask you to take these words to heart. Do not reduce them to mere mental constructs built on the relationship between Master and disciple. I am talking about innermost issues. My Ray crosses the skies of this planet and calls humans to higher service. The chosen ones can see its light. Those who sleep and who should awaken, will be roused by the roar of the thunder.

Amhaj

Contents

To the Reader

Fiery tension is necessary. It makes the flame rise and touch higher strata. The fire that burns on High is drawn down and from the fusion of the fiery streams, veils are dissolved. Thus, a new level is attained.

This book came out of inner contact with the energy of Amhaj,[1] as experienced by some individuals who devote themselves wholeheartedly to the service of the Plan of Evolution. Much more than information, it transmits impulses that stimulate the aspirant's consciousness to transcend limits... to break down barriers... to walk towards the light.

Distinctive to the closing of this cycle,[2] this book conveys the urgency of the times, helping people take on their role and recognize their dignity as particles of the great cosmos. Its words veil the Teaching and can awaken inner perceptions. Thus, may readers let go of concepts, and may they find in the impulse-ideas presented here, the portals which can lead towards wider universes.

The Consciousness which is Amhaj does not limit Itself to

---

[1] **Amhaj.** Morya and El Morya are other levels of this sublime high consciousness. The letter j is pronounced as an h: ah-mah.

[2] **This cycle.** The Earth is going through an important transition, one that will take it to a more luminous cycle, in which it will be governed by higher laws and express a life that is more in harmony with the cosmos. For this reason, the current phase is characterized by intense purification and by preparation for the rescue of those beings who chose the ways of evolution. See also Trigueirinho, *Calling Humanity* [Brazil: Irdin Editora Ltda, 2002] and other books by Trigueirinho.

the expression of a single source, but is the conduit for multiple energies that, in these times, are working for a higher development of the Earth and the kingdoms abiding on it. Those, who in the past were known as ascended Masters, members of the spiritual Hierarchy, are gathered nowadays in the planetary centers[3] or in more powerful cosmic nuclei. Thus, to associate The Voice of Amhaj with the expression of a single being would be to limit the sublime transformations which are now happening on the planet in preparation for its future stage.

You are near the Portal. The Presence will be more and more perceptible to you. But do not depend on experiences, not even elevated ones. Only faith will allow you to go beyond the veil. Yes, you have to walk alone. However, you are not on your own – you are a group. You are aware of it; so, go ahead. May your fortitude become indestructible.[4]

Trigueirinho

[3] **Planetary centers.** Energy nuclei which mediate the evolution of the planet on the manifest levels and the logoic consciousness that vivifies it. Intraterrestrial civilizations with an advanced level of development are extensions of these centers, which may also have prolongations active on the surface of the Earth. In these times the principal planetary centers are: Anu Tea, Aurora, Erks, Iberah, Lis-Fatima, Mirna Jad and Miz Tli Tlan.

[4] This fragment in italics as well as those at the beginning of each chapter and in the content of the chapters themselves, are literal transcriptions of the impulses transmitted by the Amhaj Consciousness.

1. Strands of Light

The invincibility of the spirit is not based on earthly law, but on the laws of the cosmos. That is why ascent is necessary. Ascent is based on the renovation of energy currents and for this reason the spirit penetrates the substance of fire. New currents emanate powerfully from the Great Magnet. The disciple's heart responds to the Call.

1. You are on the threshold of a new race.[1] My treasure will be revealed to you.

2. Although humanity has been informed about past races, it has learned little from its mistakes. Humans went on looking for recognition, reward and self-gratification. A stone wall would have responded more swiftly to the Call. The indolent human mass, which denies the Light and is satisfied with decaying matter, needs help but rejects it. Thus, humanity countervails wondrous possibilities. But Time regenerates time. There are those who do listen.

3. There is no time to lose. Good people hear the Call, find it beautiful, are moved by it and invite friends to discuss it. They give more importance to social meetings than to the salvation of a planet that is about to explode. But the strength of My shield will be known by those who aspire to the Most High. The power

[1] **Race.** An evolutionary stage of humanity. The development of a race is reflected in the formation of people's mental, emotional and physical-etheric bodies.

of My Ray[2] will be unveiled to those who persist. The refulgence of My fire will shine forth resplendently in those who seek it.

4. I have to speak to you in codes. You will know how to understand the true meaning of each word when you receive it into your hearts. The heart is to be cultivated as the Seed of Time. It synthesizes what is above and what is below and emits the sound. The sound awakens the fire. May you recognize the difference between an ember and a blazing flame, and love the unification. Those who have welcomed the seed of the future will no longer have to work with the dormant treasure, but they will receive their own destiny from on High. So, cast aside what has already passed.

5. That which is on High awakens and draws what is below. That which is below opens up and responds to what is on High. The midway point vibrates: there is need for fervor. There is need for love of the Law, above all else. The sublime synthesis approaches consummation. It will carry the chosen ones beyond the kingdom of death.

---

[2] **Ray.** In this context, when capitalized, the word Ray refers to one of the basic energies of the cosmos, emanations of the One Source. Seven Rays became active during the past cycle of the Earth (1st. Ray: Will-Power; 2nd Ray: Love-Wisdom; 3rd Ray: Intelligent activity; 4th Ray: Harmony; 5th Ray: Concrete Knowledge and Science; 6th Ray: Devotion and Surrender; 7th Ray: Ceremonial Order). On August 8, 1988, (8/8/88), when the planetary transition began, the other Rays became more active on the monadic level of consciousness and on the more nonmaterial levels as well. In the energy expressed by Amhaj, while the First Ray, Will-Power, is dominant, all the others are also manifested in different tones.

6. The Fire of Amhaj is ready to burst into flame. Only those who are unified with it can bear its power. It is necessary to dispel human greed that has reduced to ashes everything which should be aflame.

7. Many look to meditation in order to relax. They want the fire of heaven in their fireplaces. Furthermore, the word meditation is now obsolete. The spirit should be integrated into life; all of life should be its expression. Enter the new rhythm. The cycle has changed.

8. A spirit may live in more than one dwelling. In fact, this is what the Great Ones do. Without descending from on High, They are present in innumerable dwellings. Those around them generally do not recognize Them, which is usually a help. In silence, the Great Ones sow the Good.

9. The spirit rejuvenates as it ascends. That is how it returns to its origins. Know that you cannot proceed without fervor.

10. Power emanates from wisdom. Power emanates from love. Power is the guardian of the future. On this pathway, promises are not enough. You must go forward.

11. The ascending path is the middle way. The ascending path is forged with aspiration. The ascending path embraces invincibility. The ascending path shines. The ascending path summons the chosen ones. The ascending path redeems the past.

12. The spirit which has awakened to the light can no longer regress. Material obscureness does not attract it and only in higher spheres can it find its sustenance. But it will discover that it has woven strong ties with matter, which it will have to relinquish, and that illusion still impregnates its robes. There are some who sever those ties and ascend in their flight, penetrating higher spheres. There are also those who are afraid and keep waiting for the decay that pervades the world of form to decompose their chains. I advocate the first path, the direct way to the Kingdom. It is to this path that all who truly love are destined.

13. The power of this Ray is still unknown to most people. In the past, many cultures believed that a powerful god lived inside volcanoes. In that belief they were closer to reality than the science of today.

14. To reach liberation in this universe, the spirit can follow a straight path or venture along a crooked one. In neither case can it escape pain. In the first case, it will suffer the pain of the world and thus relieve it. In the second case, it will suffer the pain of not having responded as it ought to have done, and will suffer for its own sake. Those who are awake should be able to discern. So, do not attach yourself to what must die.

15. The grace granted to the warriors[3] helps them to overcome limitations. Warriors know the value of conquest – this is why they delve into the essence of love.

---

[3] **Warriors.** One of the hierarchical lineages. There are seven known hierarchical lineages in the Earth's ambit: Mirrors, Priests, Contemplatives, Warriors, Healers, Teachers and Rulers.

16. Do not be deceived by words, nor by the concepts you wove around them. The warrior spirit goes to battle, not because it likes fighting, but because justice is the blade of its sword.

17. Because of their paltriness, human beings applied the concept of conquest to material life. Overcome by greed they sought to dominate others and thus they strayed from the true path.

18. There is no external security. Even so, humans insist on looking for it. They have not yet realized that life goes on in continuous transformation. The succession of images presented by the senses is no more than a tiny aspect of a greater reality which transcends the mental world and touches supraphysical reality. A turtle may feel safe by carrying its house on its back – but it cannot fly.

19. Life resides within form, but transcends it. Form comes out of the movement of Life and tends towards crystallization. The disciple of the law must not be confused by the appearance of events.

20. One of the tasks of disciples is to overcome and transcend the ancestral forces which impregnate their bodies. It is not easy to live in a dark well without touching the mud. However, this is what they must do. And they will do so when they realize that they must not walk on the ground, but in the air.

21. Many people amuse themselves with the Teaching. They do not recognize the depth of what is being transmitted to them. Others think that by reading an inspired book they no longer

need to work at transforming themselves. They flaunt spiritual sayings. They even change the way they dress! They are like whitewashed tombs. Transfiguration does not occur from the outside in. Its foundation must be forged by the disciple, not on the surface but through real transformations.

22. Disciples love transcendence but do not expose themselves to danger. They know they must take care of the chalice that has been entrusted to them.

23. Covetousness is deeply ingrained in human consciousness. This evil must be rooted out. From the beginning of time this planet has sheltered dark entities, but in this way other regions of the cosmos have been preserved from the attacks of these forces. This is why the Earth will be redeemed. This is why the Time of Samana's[4] presence has come. This is why the power of Amhaj's sword will be revealed to the Earth.

24. The light of the stars may be hidden behind clouds, but it is still there. Disciples must learn to be connected to those worlds of pure light, regardless of atmospheric conditions. In fact, they must learn to be in those worlds, to live in them while fulfilling tasks on Earth. It is possible. It is achieved by ardent aspiration.

25. By analogy, the knowledge of canal building that brought many practical benefits to terrestrial humanity should be applied to other levels of existence. Everything in the cosmos is interconnected; however, this linking is transformed at each level.

[4] **Samana.** Sublime entity which governs the intergalactic operation for rescue and salvation of the Earth.

Disciples know that the manifestations of life are relative to specific spheres, thus they act accordingly.

26. Love the Truth. Power should arise from deep within you and permeate your labor – the power to persist... the power to love... the power to be just... the power to manifest the light.

27. My Ray leads you to transfiguration. My Ray leads you to span frontiers. My Ray leads you to the essence. It tears apart but does not wound; it demolishes and thus opens up pathways. We are casting the mold of the new human. We are laying the foundations of a new civilization. Evil must be rooted out. The light that is approaching the Earth must be wholeheartedly embraced.

28. I bring you the impulse of the new law. The disciple understands inwardly that even the sublime spheres are taut. The whole galaxy is undergoing a profound transition. I call this tension the Preparation for the Encounter; it attracts the most beautiful configurations.

29. The capacity for rebirth is part of this Ray, but only during the initial phases of the path. Disciples will realize that beyond the successive cycles of birth and death lies continuous transcendence, and they head towards it. My Ray will accompany them. It is called the Guardian of the Future.

30. Disciples recognize that true existence occurs in the cosmos; the materiality of their bodies does not hinder the flight of consciousness. However, they know that matter must be refined.

So they work with the highest fires, making it possible for translucency to emerge. Redemption is based on this intrinsic quality in matter, a quality that allows it to reveal its essential purity. Disciples are called those-who-reveal-Beauty. This they have learned to do for they have already gone beyond the initial veils.

31. The beauty of incandescent metal is nothing compared with the flaming armor of the awakened spirit. With its fiery vibration, this spirit regenerates form and so form becomes dissolved in the essence that generated it. The strength of the spirit is based in the power of the sublime spheres, which are rooted in the cosmic source of love. Through grace, the Master elevates the disciple, and thus the disciple can bathe in the Source. Through grace, the disciple is taken before the Great Mirror[5] where the mysteries of Creation are revealed. Through grace, the disciple transcends limitations, and thus gratefully welcomes the tasks which are given by the Most High.

32. Many people cross the desert, but not all reach their destination. This calls for determination, firmness, moderation and faith. Those who venture along the pathway of light must cross this region of consciousness and learn lessons from its mysteries. One cannot go forward without crossing frontiers. This is why

---

[5] **Mirror.** A nucleus of energies that is part of the subtle network of cosmic communication. Mirrors transmit energies which permeate all manifested life. Certain specific qualities of the aura on all levels of consciousness determine whether or not a nucleus, such as a planet, a civilization, a group or an individual, is a mirror. All beings are directly or indirectly in touch with this network of mirrors, but only some are a part of its circuits. The term mirror-being designates souls that are dedicated to this particular work of receiving and reflecting energies in a pure way. See Trigueirinho, *Calling Humanity* [op. cit.], pages 25-26.

My Ray brings you the power to transform, to liberate and to transcend. This is why My Ray emerges, shattering fetters.

33. Magnificent power permeates consciousness and awakens it. Magnificent power penetrates matter and tears its veils. Magnificent power elevates the being and transmutes it into Light. Yes, the freedom of the spirit vibrates in the innermost core of the being.

34. The spirit develops different aspects of evolution during specific phases of its ascesis. Those phases cannot be avoided, but they can be surpassed all together. Currrently the rays[6] emanated by different spheres blend into a single ray, thus strengthening one another. Stars reach maximum brilliance before being quickly absorbed into their center, likewise the Flaming Power flares up and imprints the sign of the new race on the material sphere. It is time to glorify the Supreme – not with promises, but with self-surrender. My Mantle will be your protection.

35. I proclaim the forthcoming of the new human. I proclaim the forthcoming of the new race. I proclaim the forthcoming of the new civilization. The power of the cosmos infuses the earthly sphere. With this power We build the foundations of the future. Do not confuse these words with the atrocities of your civilization. This is not the power of domination, the act of dark forces, but rather it is the power of the Good. Therefore, I affirm the victory of the light.

---

[6] **Rays.** When not capitalized, the word rays simply refers to the emanations of energy and not to one of the twelve cosmic Rays.

36. The hero sublimated his existence through the action of fire. Ardent aspiration opens the doors of the future; this is why it belongs to this Ray. Ascent is not possible without this aspiration that leads to greater accomplishments. Those related to darkness, walk in darkness. The disciple of the law enters the Great Light.

37. Many wonder why We so often repeat an instruction. They do not realize that in the Teaching there is no repetition. It is generally necessary to play the same note, but each time the attuned ear will pick up new harmonic sounds and rejoice in the beauty of the cosmos. Beauty is hidden in simplicity; the fiery path is hidden in the fulfillment of the law. Those who tire of apparent repetitions are immature and have yet to put the first lessons into practice.

38. Many were visited by Our Messengers but never even listened to them! They preferred the smells of earthly existence to the subtle aroma of celestial jasmines. Value the opportunities that are being offered to you. Before night falls, the Messenger will be at your door.

39. The keys to understanding the Teaching are found in perfecting one's character and in surrendering oneself to the Most High. One does not need intellectualism to penetrate the mysteries of the Teaching, but only purity and faith. Intellectuals nourish themselves with ashes of the past. The pure ones share the wisdom of the heavenly spheres.

40. Fish cannot fly, but they can descend into ever deeper

waters. To each one is given a sphere and also the way to transcend it. But most humans keep moving ahead slowly within the vibration of material evolution. Those who advance firmly and cross frontiers know the power of My Ray. The magnificence of this Ray is not disclosed to the lukewarm, but to those who daringly take up the Sword of the Law. They are the chosen ones; within the invisible they were able to find the doorway to ascent.

41. Some disciples are active in the planetary sphere. Others are learning to touch the solar sphere. However, most follow the way by serving in groups. All are being especially stimulated in these times. There is no particle that has not received the touch of My Ray. Responses to it vary greatly: from denial and tepidness to the fervent *yes*. Those who answer affirmatively, receive a new impulse and can enter wider spheres. In the cosmos, everything happens according to the law of affinity. Those who truly love, understand the mystery of magnetic resonance.

42. Most disciples work on subtle levels, but few actually fulfill tasks in the concrete stratum of the material world. The training to act on the physical level is rigorous and their bodies cannot always bear the required tension. Those who can clearly support planetary service externaly are rare. They are jewels we hold close to Our heart. Many opportunities are being created in these times, but We know that not all the seeds which are sown will sprout.

2. Keys of the future

You should not envisage the battle. The Master will determine each encounter. Confrontation is necessary to produce ardent tension without which you cannot ascend.

1. "Let the little ones come to me," the Teacher told you in the past. Yes, purity manifests Our Path with perfection. It is the sign of this Brotherhood.

2. Many students, when hearing that purity is needed, dress themselves in white, forgetting that true dispassion lies within. They flaunt this banner, but carry the dust of this civilization on their shoes. May you know that it is time for the new human to be born. It is time to really undertake transformation. One cannot build the new world based on casual promises. Matter must be permeated by fire and transformed, poured into the mold of redemption. Therefore, I summon you to imprint on each act of your life the determination to transcend. Love this fire. On this path you will have Our blessing.

3. Distance does not hinder your contact with Us. The disciple has already learned this. But now the moment has come for many aspirants who tread the path of light to cross the First Portal. May they persevere. May they surpass the trials. May they learn to walk on fire.

4. Our Envoys have carefully cultivated the seed of the new human. It began to be formed thousands of years ago, according to chronological time of the terrestrial sphere. The preparation of the soil to receive this seed also began a long time ago. Nevertheless, few humans have a consciousness that is ready to receive it. But this is not the most important. Two humans would suffice for the new humanity to become established on the planet.

5. Terrestrial humanity has not learned the mysteries of the progression of energy. It stopped at the first steps, not wanting to listen to the Teaching. We have always been present, showing humanity the path, but no one is compelled to respond. On this path, it is necessary to acquiesce. I am not talking of the response of the external consciousness, but of the *yes* that must sound in the celestial worlds. After all, one must want to return Home.

6. Existence in the more subtle planes of the terrestrial sphere is beginning to be unveiled. Pathways of the new Earth are disclosed in glimpses. The new Earth already exists on higher planes and I tell you, it is not far from the material sphere. An important stage of this coming is being experienced these days, for a delicate threshold has been reached: the concrete strata must be dissolved in light and must welcome future life. This is why many changes are taking place and why the Call is sounding intensely once again. Disciples should keep this in mind and refine their attunement. The flow of the Great Current must not be interrupted.

7. Some students, on hearing about the birthing of the new humanity, get side-tracked by details, digress into flights of their imagination, and hence lose the essence of the Teaching. The color of the eyes or of the skin of future humans is not important, but rather the level of their consciousness. Those who follow the ascending path must now seek that level. Hence We say: the new Earth already exists on the higher spheres of the planet. It is the task of the servers of Light to bring it into manifestation.

8. Countless ties bind terrestrial humanity to the past. Those ties must be broken for the spirit to ascend. Much can be done consciously by humanity itself, but the transition is only possible through the action of Grace. Yes, the time has come to love freedom. The time has come to be free.

9. The birthing of a race occurs within the light of sublime spheres and goes on being reflected through the successive levels of planetary life, until it penetrates the darkness of matter. An immeasurable network of energies, beings and consciousnesses, participates in this process. My Ray is present therein, as guardian of the new portal.

10. It is incredible how even the best people tend to ignore the sublimity of life and remain in pettiness. This tendency frequently creeps into the highest aspirations. Therefore, I recommend vigilance and, above all, self-surrender. The first step is to understand and accept the warning. The next step is to live it.

11. Sacredness will be restored by the new human. Everything in life will be recognized as a gift, and a means to glorify the Creator. However, one should not wait until tomorrow to manifest that which is new. Sacredness, above all, should be lived now. Hence, may reverence prevail.

12. Those who persist will see the light of the new dawn. Those who persist will discover the power of winged conquest. Those who persist will unveil the sign of Our Brotherhood. Yes, the battle must be taken on. Raise the sword and affirm the law.

13. The new cannot be built by using old patterns. This is a time of mutations; hence intensifying the currents is so beautiful. All the colors merge to form the new order. The joy of encountering the light permeates the higher spheres. This rejoicing should penetrate material darkness and within it, light up the flame of Our Ray.

14. Can a bird soar in lofty flights inside a little cage? Certainly not. But for the spirit there are no such limitations. This is why I affirm that those who listen to the Call can really fly. Even if submerged in the material spheres, in consciouness they can soar to the Infinite.

15. There are no mysteries to fulfilling the law. And fulfilling the law could transform the Earth into a heavenly kingdom! So why does humanity insist on evading this task? The answer is easy: like attracts like. Because of free will the most beautiful opportunities are lost.

16. The slaughter of animals goes on in spite of all Our warnings. Do humans not perceive the undesirable visitors that are attracted by such viciousness? All you have to do is to look at the daily news to realize that humanity itself sows the violence of the world.

17. For the new Earth to be manifested on the material level it is necessary to first settle all accounts. Some disciples are even impressed by the speed with which those adjustments are being made. This is why one must sharpen one's attunement. This is why one must be unreservedly united to the Good.

18. Many have already noticed changes in the flow of time and also in the density of some material objects. Transformations of the human body itself are also perceptible, especially in the blood plasma. However, in the midst of so much fog, these discoveries are considered to be mistakes, and humankind remains tied to old patterns. May the pioneers know how to read the signs. May they not get lost. May they love the Law.

19. Today the terrestrial sphere requires great attention. The currents are so strong that special measures are needed to keep them in balance. The assaults of the enemy are continuous; but Our stronghold is invincible. The new human exists as a pattern to be manifested on the future Earth and the new race will not be contaminated by the odor of the present civilization. Victory is certain but time is growing short. The battle has not yet ended.

20. The seed of a new race is being cultivated concurrently on several vibratory levels. The planetary sphere, like a huge laboratory, welcomes this sublime process. It is true, that depending on the present stage, only certain regions will offer the right conditions for this chemistry to take place. The conscious collaboration of humanity of the surface has so far been minimal, but the Brothers of Space have always been present and their action is still essential. As builders of the new times, they bring the most precious combinations of rays of light from the cosmos. May you welcome the new seed.

21. The role of the rings of Saturn is mysterious to terrestrial humanity. Several theories have been built on this subject, but none of them has been able to unveil reality. There are many correspondences between the functioning of the human body and the Earth's interaction with neighboring worlds. However, Our Envoys withdrew the keys of this science long ago to safeguard it from being beleaguered by the imprudent. But nowadays, in the midst of humanity, there are those who can bear the forceful power of fire from space. They are being given the Torch of Knowledge. They are bearers of light.

22. Some have called the Earth "the blue planet." We used to call it the "imprisoned planet." But now the situation is changing and the new Earth is getting ready to emerge. Instead of prisoner, this little planet will become a base for the ascending spirit. Its task is important, more than you can possibly imagine. Ask Sirius. This star will answer you in secret.

23. Archeological research has revealed very little about the true past of humanity. In the etheric records one may find correct information about its trajectory as well as the possibilities for its future. Humankind lost the keys for contacting those luminous records when it chose to merge into the density of the material plane beyond what was envisaged. Everything has its price. But throughout time there have been those who, united to Our Brotherhood, could act as transmitters of the Teaching. They gleaned from these records the information they needed to accomplish their tasks. Now much more can be revealed and the disciples are being silently prepared for this.

24. The rays of Jupiter have not yet been detected by earthly medical science; but today many cures happen through their action. Furthermore, because of them, some infectious diseases are worsened when impurities have not been adequately removed. Such impurities are of psychic origin and are projected on to the materiality of the bodies. Therefore, we say that treatments must not be limited to the physical vehicle, but the causes for distortions must be sought in the invisible worlds.

25. Many students ask themselves how to recognize and use the rays that emanate from the planets and stars. This is knowledge that cannot be acquired through studies. It comes through the perfect interaction of their consciousness with the essence of the ray. This is why We advocate self-surrender as the path towards the truth. From self-surrender come the benefits for the service of the world.

26. In the future civilization the rays sent to Earth from the cosmos will be correctly understood and widely used, including in harmonizing beings and bodies. As you have already been informed, some experiments are occurring in this field as a preparation for the new life – not in earthly laboratories, but in space vessels.

27. The rays of Venus have a unique tone and vibration. Silently they elevate consciousness, allowing it to become permeated by balms of compassion and wisdom. It is beautiful to see flowers blossoming in this garden. It is beautiful to see the Earth becoming reintegrated into the cosmos.

28. Many people have a relatively active inner life but are unaware of it. Immersed in presumed duties, they forget to turn to the Source of Light that is within them. They must learn the correct measure of facts and values. One cannot go on wasting one's entire incarnation time and time again.

29. For the seed to germinate, it must be sown in adequate soil. Furthermore, it should be protected until it has become well rooted. There are people who think they are ready to receive the seed of the new human in their consciouness, but pride prevents them from living it fully. There are others who, with feelings of inferiority, close their doors to this sowing and thus curtail their own potential. Thus, selflessness is the best path. It is a narrow path and can only be trodden by surrendering the ego to the Master. Harken to these words for they hold the key to your liberation.

30. You cannot yet perceive the magnificence of these times, although by the vision of the spirit you can go beyond the atrocities committed by this civilization. What really matters, brothers, is the light which is now being liberated by the purifying flame, and not the soot from that fire. Light – sign of the coming times.

31. When overcome by grief, offer it up to the Most High. When overwhelmed by disillusion, give thanks and surrender yourself to the Supreme. When weighed down by dryness, bless it, for it announces luminous times when you will be working closer to Us.

32. What really matters is the cosmic path of the being, not the movement of the forms in the terrestrial sphere. To grasp this you need to have a correct sense of proportion. Your whole existence cannot be based only on a small fraction of it. From the very beginning of time We have sounded the Call, but humanity has not wanted to hear it. Now harvest time has arrived. There is no further way to postpone the sublime coming. Therefore, We say: glory to the heavens; blessed is the One who comes in the name of the Lord.

33. My sword cuts the air and announces the new times. My sword shatters the darkness and opens the way for the light. Its thin edge is the path of the chosen, of those who answered the Call and persevered. All may tread the path of evolution. The love of the cosmos offers its gifts to everyone. Balance must be maintained in the universes and therefore each being must settle

accounts before departing. In this end of cycle, the surface of the Earth will be a stage of horrors. May the lessons be learned and may this universe nevermore return to darkness.

34. If We could, We would cancel the heavy requiting blow which looms over humanity and the planet. But for the spirit to be liberated the fetters must be broken. Thus, purification accompanies the closing of accounts. The sky darkens when the storm breaks. Yet, when it is over, deep peace pervades. Our disciples are called the Sowers of the Future for in the midst of darkness they herald Peace.

35. Today the whole solar system turns towards the Earth in a special way – not only the solar system, but also a great part of the cosmos. When delicate surgery is needed, all efforts are focused on the ailing organ. May you know that evil has been overcome. But time must take its course so that the enemies' armies may first settle their accounts with one another.

36. What is worth more – a material or a sentimental loss or the liberation of the spirit? Certainly the latter. Moreover, the former is frequently an instrument for this liberation. So one must maintain the correct attitude towards the events of life, and above all, fervently aspire to the Good. The Will of the Spirit shall permeate human will. May it be so for the Supreme Glory.

37. Your integration with Our Brotherhood happens in the kingdom of the spirit. This kingdom is Consciousness, and so the student should abstain from seeking phenomenal experiences.

The material sphere is too dense to receive the rhythm of light and so all matter of the planet must urgently ascend. Such times of tribulation need those who pray. These selfless members of terrestrial humanity are to devote themselves to the light. Much more can be done through them to redeem the human past than by the intervention of other humanities.[1] You know the law of karma.[2] You will find the reasons for this in the law of karma.

38. When the sky darkens during the day and the light can no longer be seen, keep still and pray. Give thanks, for the moment of the great liberation will have arrived. Strengthen your link with the Hierarchy. Strengthen your unification with supreme love. Do not fear. The spirit rejoices in liberation.

39. You have given Our Messengers different names, but it is time to recognize Them as a single shaft of light. The Brotherhood of the cosmos is an expression of the supreme unity and your being should unite with it. Like a flaming link, bind your consciousness to the Almighty.

40. Terrestrials refer to the planets as celestial bodies. This is not completely wrong, but it has limitations. It is better to call them states of consciousness and in many cases, schools for humanity. The time is coming when human beings will be

---

[1] **Other humanities.** Humanities that live in other dimensions, such as the intra-terrestrial, intra-oceanic and extraterrestrial dimensions.

[2] **Law of karma.** The law of cause and effect. The law of karma in the material realm, decrees that each action generates an effect that, in time, becomes the cause of a following effect. It acts in such a way as to equilibrate the universes. It can be described in the biblical terms: [...] man reaps what he sows. See also: Trigueirinho, *Beyond Karma* [Brazil: Irdin Editora Ltda., 2003].

able to project themselves freely beyond the terrestrial sphere and find their kin in other schools as well. Fullness is their destiny. Therefore, I tell you: in your spirit you have the keys to the future.

41. Readiness is necessary for Our disciples. The task is given to them, but they have to decode Our message. The success of the task depends on their attunement. They should have already learned this. Creativity abides in the perfection of the spirit; the link with Our current is to be found in obedience to the law. In other words, there is no way to overcome the enemy without being linked to the Source.

42. The fire blazes in the higher spheres. The next stage of the planet is ready to emerge on the surface of the Earth as well. What has so often been announced will be manifested.

3. Sparks of Awakening

The blue flame traveled through infinite universes and hid a sacred seed in the Earth. The seed is now beginning to germinate. Open your heart and welcome its invisible presence.

1. You know how importat it is to remain attuned with Us. Without this firm connection the service cannot be deepened. The Hierarchy kindles the flame of awakening; the Great Flow spreads Its blessings over those who respond to the Call. May those who can hear, follow Its signs. The Earth must be elevated and the time is now.

2. Gone is the time of lethargy, darkness and dubious pacts. It is no longer possible to remain undecided. May aspirants know which master they are serving.

3. If you seek the light, surrender to it. Do not delude yourselves. You need firmness and loyalty. The keys to power will be given to those who cross the Portal. May the servers go forward. May they know the value of surrender; may they truly love.

4. Our power instructs. Our power redeems. Our power governs the life of the spirit. The plant kingdom has beautifully recognized the power of the light. May humanity learn the lesson of humility from these fellow creatures.

5. Not always can disciples accurately grasp the message transmitted to them. There are so many emanations from the intermediate spheres that it is often necessary to wait for the atmosphere to clear up. This is why We indicate purity as the basis for unification with the higher currents. May the disciples watch over their emanations. Thought and desire determine the attunement.

6. I have much to tell you, but the instructions must be transmitted gradually. We are weaving a delicate mantle. We cannot let the threads get entangled. Fervor, as well as continual renewal of vows, is needed for this work. My energy and yours must be correctly interwoven – they will merge and will become a single expression. The work will be manifested with each woven thread. Be not anxious, but ready.

7. Devotion is the flame that sustains pilgrims on the path and carries them forward. May it be pure. And may the pilgrims know how to die to what has passed.

8. Devotion and humility are the basis for surrender. Reverence is born from the union of those currents. Delicate seeds are germinating; the planet is rapidly becoming transformed. Take up the path with sincerity.

9. The disciples have surrendered their existence to the Master. The Master and the essence of the disciple are one and the same life. How can the mind grasp such a sublime union? Only in the kingdom of the spirit can one be aware of the links in this chain.

10. Devotion is a foundation of existence in the sublime spheres. All the particles there vibrate glorifying the Creator. Devotion is rooted in the Ray of Power. Thus, it leads the spirit along the path of continuous transcendence. The disciple is instructed to seek devotion within and cultivate it with purity. What a beautiful Call echoes through the skies of the planet! May those who are to ascend hear this call.

11. The flame of life is eternal, but its radiance varies according to the environment. So, We recommend continual affirmation of inner vows. The links with the Hierarchy must be strengthened. Heaven and Earth must become one. Supreme love must permeate all the particles. It is time to awaken.

12. The energies of the various spheres interrelate like instruments in an orchestra. There are moments when only one must play; there are others in which the sounds of several instruments intermingle. There are also rare occasions when all of them play the chords of the symphony together. The Great Regent conducts everything, knows everything, and observes everything. Be assured that all is under control: the new Earth will emerge and show its true face.

13. Life on the surface of the planet will be transfigured. This process has already begun. So I beg you to be firmly and steadfastly determined to proceed on the Way. Nurture the flame of faith in your heart and in the hearts of your fellow beings. Heed this advice and be vigilant; go forward.

14. Faith – tiny word but powerful enough to transfigure all existence.

15. The manifestation of the universes is founded on precise laws, some of which you already know. You must not only register them mentally, but also live them in their higher expression. For some people this process happens consciously, and thus the celestial signs are molded in the material world.

16. On each level of a universe, the governing laws are expressed in different ways. The disciple is asked to recognize each one of them, and step by step, to reach the Source.

17. Like the laws, the energies unfold into an infinity of expressions. They mark out spans within which beings evolve. To cross the limits of a specific span means to contact new energies and new laws. The Earth has been isolated from the cosmos, but now it is to become reintegrated. For this, my Ray is present.

18. One must understand correctly the meaning of the word *power*. This understanding does not emerge until consciousness has gone beyond certain veils and has found, deep within, the source of the love which is wisdom. In this universe power comes from love. In wider spheres, one realizes that love comes from the supreme power.

19. Cosmic existence is infinite; its manifestation immeasurable. The doors to other universes are now open to beings from this planet and relocations are already occurring. The required attitudes are: absence of attachement and of expectations. Each one has his or her own path. For once and for all, may terrestrial understanding learn to bow before the wisdom of the cosmos.

20. Can the wind and the rains obey human commands? Certainly. However, this must happen in harmony with the universe of which they are part, and not according to human whims or prejudices. Cooperation with other kingdoms will be part of the future life of this humanity and I assure you, the time is not far off when it will occur openly.

21. The hierarchy of the devas encompasses multiple echelons and thirteen basic classes of elementals. The integration of these kingdoms with humans is necessary for the development of the Earth, but it will only be manifested widely after the purification of material levels. The increasing subtleness of human consciouness, as well as the mediation of the devas between humankind and the elementals, are necessary for this integration to take place. You will see miracles in the present planetary transition, but they will be no more than a tiny part of the fullness that awaits the planet.

22. As consciousness expands, the future draws closer to the present. Manifold possibilities have always existed, but to be externalized, each link in the chain of manifestation has to bear the resulting tension. Yes, humanity and Hierarchy must become unified for the terrestrial world to ascend.

23. We approach the disciples at the right moment, therefore there is no reason for them to vacillate. We grant them the opportunities to act so that they may become skilled in self-control and in channeling energy for the task at hand. Each one has a role in the manifestation of the great mosaic – the Plan of Evolution. This is why each particle that lights up in response to Our call is

so important.

24. Even though they know the laws that govern spiritual life, many students do not practice them. This is understandable, but not justifiable. Whoever seeks the light should express this commitment in thought, in feeling and in action. It is an inner commitment between consciousness and its Source. Irrevocable, there is no way to evade it. Sooner or later, the particles of light will return to the Central Flame. So why postpone the luminous future and delay the progress of the entire flow? Great is the responsibility of those who are able to advance towards the light but choose the shadows! This is why the karmic plot of this planet is so dismal.

25. Do not look for culprits. Each one is responsible for his or her own acts. These is inevitable. The laws that hold the universes in balance are applied with a precision beyond human imagination. Thus We say: transform in yourselves that which has to be transformed in the world. Elevate in yourselves that which has to be elevated on this Earth. Truly love the light.

26. "Know thyself." This key was given to humankind long ago and very few have actually used it. But, there is no other way to return Home.

27. In trying to know themselves, humans have plunged into a dark well instead of turning towards the Most High. They have kept on rotating around their own ego instead of ascending to the origin of the self. They have worked with the shadows instead

of seeking the source of light. There is no time to lose. Go firmly ahead. Time is running out and truth is pressing to be expressed on material levels. And this time is coming.

28. The universes are consecrated through the fulfillment of laws. In applying its governing laws to perfection, the entire universe lights up as a result of its own radiance. Such magnificence cannot be described in earthly terms. The fire of space is all-embracing and its splendor is only revealed to those who transcend their own level of being. We say: "Go onward!"

29. In times such as these, what is the use of getting caught up in the chronicle of events of this civilization? You would be of more help to the world if you conquered the enemy within yourself. Earnestly ask for grace – and it will be granted to you.

30. The Hierarchy blesses all those who sincerely turn to Them. However, you will approach Them according to your own openness. Therefore, do not try to maneuver Our transmissions. The greatest treasures are given to those who want nothing. May these words be heeded, since those who are predestined are sleeping instead of moving onward.

31. There will always be a higher law to be recognized, applied, fully lived – and then transcended. You know that evolution is infinite. However, on this path it is not enough merely to have information; it is necessary to transform it into an instrument for ascending. Indescribable is the power of the flame that links reverence for the Supreme with daring. The mysteries of existence are unveiled to those who penetrate and are absorbed

by this fire. For them, the firmament is transformed into a flaming canopy and they move along it. We welcome the daring ones – those who love.

32. Ascent is the pathway of the law. The power which attracts all particles towards the Origin is inscrutable to humankind. This power emanates from the Central Fire and subsists in the core of Creation. My Ray manifests this power and thus it will be more and more active in these times. It heralds eternity. It reveals to humankind the fiery path of the spirit. Summon those who thirst for Life. I will show them the way to the Source.

33. Few on this planet really know silence. However, the changes that could come from it are powerful. Silence is necessary to understand universal laws and to accomplish the task correctly. Silence is the vestibule for the Encounter. To enter into silence one must have devotion; one must have purity and faith.

34. The law of equilibrium governs everything; it permeates all existence. It is present in the pulsation of all particles. It manifests itself in different ways and acts on various spheres, but always leads beings to self-fulfillment. The mysteries of the cosmos are contained in this law. Disciple, delve deeply into it and you will recognize your true face.

35. Immortality is the path of the chosen. Through it they will some day arrive at the immutable existence. But do not think there is an end to this journey. Infinite, it requires courage.

Courage is an attribute of My Ray, which presently opens pathways to the new Earth. May you value life in all spheres. All of them are part of the great cosmos; all must shine.

36. There is no real difference between small and great actions. Erroneous concepts created by human beings overlay reality, covering it with absurdity. In fact, any kind of movement reverberates through the immensity of the cosmos and is reflected in the different spheres. It is time for you to be aware of your contribution to the integration of the universes. After all, you have to mature.

37. Devotion frees one from even the heaviest chains. Like the fiery flame consuming matter, it leads the pilgrim along the infinite path. How many gifts humankind has refused! But spirit is tireless and grows stronger in battle. Do not postpone your arrival even further.

38. Much of what was considered achievement and goal in the past has become less important today. So, you can hardly imagine the future of the planet, since you have no reference for it. The Earth holds a precious treasure. The stars know it. Together, Orion, Betelgeuse and Sirius chant new canticles. Hasten, and learn from them the key of the new symphony.

39. Stars, beloved sisters... in silence you guard the portal of the Great Dwelling. Welcome these little ones, born on Earth, who wish to reach the heavens. Send your rays through space, to be the pathway, the protection and the reassurance of those who surrender to the light for the sake of love.

40. Be still. You have My presence. You have the protection of My Mantle shielding you. Fear nothing. Love. Abide in your heart.

41. Tendencies inherited from many generations bind consciousness firmly to material density. But it is necessary to overcome this obstacle, to tear away the veils that hide the light. Temperance is part of the pathway towards the spirit. On this path the traveler should know that all needs will be provided. The level of contact will depend on one's attunement, so keep the inner flame alight. May its radiance increase and may it enkindle the Good.

42. The Earth cannot be regenerated as long as humanity remains limited to material laws. The sacred lotus grows out of the mire, but its archetype subsists in the sublime spheres. Therefore, the key, the energy and the power to transform that which is below, are to be found on High. We have given the disciples the seeds to be sown in the soil of this planet. We have entrusted this task to them. We have shown them the way. May they not forget the value of what was given to them. May they keep vigil over the seedlings.

4. Dawn

The Sun is always present, but its light cannot be perceived in the same way, at the same time, in all regions of the planet. Cycles and phases are manifestations in the concrete spheres. However, on higher levels, serene bliss reigns – an ocean of pure consciousness, the infinite source of love and power. You are invited to enter into this mystery. Recognize yourself as an essence. You are whole. In plenitude will you live.

1. Human consciousness need not be limited to the environs of this solar system. It should expand, reach distant universes and merge into their energies. Such a journey is not taken in rockets, but in spirit. Our space vessels are live manifestations of consciousness. They are light. For them, time and space have no limits. If humans knew the immensity that awaits them perhaps they would be more willing to follow the law. The law abides in one's inner self. Therefore, frontiers are first transcended within so that later they may be transcended in material life. Terrestrial life cries out for freedom. In response to this plea, We are present and active. Build your fortress with the unassailable energy of the spirit. For this, you have My Ray. This is why you know My Name.

2. Each planet corresponds to a stage of universal evolution. No two planets are alike, nor two individuals. Cosmic creativity is infinite and reveals its power in manifold forms. Terrestrial matter is already undergoing transubstantiation, but it needs vastness to evolve. This vastness is the fruit of purity and thus all

the corners of the Earth will be cleansed. My Ray is active in this process, opening the pathway to eternity. The future is as near to you as breathing. The chronology of events is no more than a conditioning that is surpassed as soon as consciousness penetrates the spiritual kingdom. Hence, We invite you to give wings to your heart and soar toward the Infinite.

3. The density currently prevailing in the terrestrial sphere hinders one from perceiving the rays of the planets and stars. However, these rays are always present and active, like the Sun on a cloudy day. The disciple should rise above the clouds and contact these rays, recognizing their different vibrations. Learn how to attune to them and transmit them to the material plane. The training takes place under Our supervision. Self-surrender and detachment are necessary for this. A chalice must be emptied in order to be filled; a bell must be free of sediment to vibrate fully when sounded. Glorious times are coming; the planet must be prepared for them.

4. In these times the rays of Jupiter are easier to detect than those of other planets. This is due to the emergence of My Ray on the material plane. The planetary and stellar action in the terrestrial sphere is presently coordinated by the center of the Sun. The Sun is the regent of the system and sublime consciousnesses are present within its aura. This system and other points of the galaxy are linked and the unification of inter-systemic currents is a reality. The live presence of far-away stars may be perceived on Earth – the children of the stars are among Us. Our Brotherhood does not spare any effort to accomplish the task and We invite you to participate in this Work. To merge into this current one

must have fervor, readiness, surrender and faith. The spirit does all the rest.

5. The experience with rays of the planets is just beginning for this humanity. This experience takes place mainly on the subtle planes, even though its effects are clearly perceptible in the concrete world. Saturn is a school for the priests of the law, while Jupiter prepares masterful governors. The Earth should be a field for healers – this statement conceals the key of its connection with Venus. In the past Mars formed invaluable warriors, but its essence is now being transferred to other spheres. Mercury will penetrate the secrets of the Sun, as this system will no longer need the Messenger. Each planet keeps distinct connections with the cosmic universe and its mirrors reflect the rays of multiple constellations. When you are given information it refers to a specific set of circumstances, so We recommend flexibility and detachment. Some students think that the Teaching is contradictory; they do not understand that it presents different storeys of the same building. Therefore, once again We say: go deep into the fiery path. You will find the instructions you need within you.

6. Some humans have already crossed the frontiers of the Sun, even though humanity as a whole has remained prisoner of the planet. Here you have a key: the terrestrial circle was insurmountable for those human beings who were prisoners of the Earth, but not for those who knew how to fly. This Teaching has always been transmitted to the few elect who, in silence, followed the path of the Initiations. The Earth is opening its doors to neighboring universes because the freedom of the future has been assured by the Councils. This is why these times are precious

and We can more widely unveil realities which once were hidden. Those who can hear, will understand.

7. Much of what We transmitted to you in the past is no longer valid today. The Teaching was not wrong, but human consciousness has expanded and can now encompass a broader view. Those who have penetrated the aura of Truth know that Its essence is untouchable. The closer one comes to this essence, the deeper it gets. Thus, flexibility and detachment are again recommended. To follow the ascent of the spirit one must be dynamic.

8. Truth is relative to the boundaries of one's consciousness. Thus, the awakened pilgrim always renews his or her standards. No matter how beautiful the weaving might be, the genuine artisan is never satisfied.

9. Long have We drawn your attention to the intensity of the battle. Now I tell you: much has happened, but the conflict has not yet come to an end. What took place on the subtle spheres will plunge down upon Earth. However, the one whose forbearance comes from the spirit recognizes the power of the Hierarchy. The urn will be shattered and the essence therein will be spread over the entire planet. Thus, Good is drawn forth from evil.

10. Those who perceive the coming of the new times should hasten and manifest the new sign in external life. May they not yield to the beckoning of the enemy. May they follow the law. May they be attentive. Through the fire of love, may they sustain their link with the Hierarchy.

11. Fiery progression exponentially fuels the power of those who firmly answer the Call. Their flaming armor is fortified under the onslaught of the enemy's arrows. Their determination heralds the new Earth. But there are those who did not want to recognize the urgency of these times. They preferred the lethargy of a sick civilization in which even the best standards are interwoven with darkness. I call you to ardent conquest. I call you to service. I speak your Name. Come, O Children of the Sun!

12. Do not look for rewards. In the ascending path the worm of retribution becomes ever fainter, until it is definitively expelled from the aura of the being. To eradicate it, We recommend silence and humility. Moreover, the pilgrim is to walk on, without looking back.

13. The inappropriate intermingling of vibrations, so common on your planet in these days, must be promptly replaced by a magnetic selectivity. The capacity to do so is developed through aspiration, surrender and, above all, discernment. Discernment is born from the fusion of the energies in the centers of the head and the heart; hence, the need for silence. Recognize the importance of rhythm and correctly conduct the strands of light that the Hierarchy sends you.

14. The power of selfless action is immeasurable. Its radiation crosses frontiers and reaches the most distant universes. Now that the final moments of this cycle are drawing near on the material plane, horror will take over the stage of human life. Pure faith and selflessness are needed. The spirit is immortal, but one must allow it to ascend.

15. Up to now the mantle of life on the surface of the Earth has been woven with threads of grief and suffering. Through their choices people were able to learn to tell the bad from the good and the good from the right. But now it is necessary to change the woven pattern, and for this reason you are living moments of intense trials. No longer grief and suffering, but a firm determination to advance will trace the pattern of this weaving.

16. There have always been those who devoted their lives entirely to the Supreme Lord of the universes. They opened pathways for humanity; they were pillars of strength sustaining the planet. This total dedication is the sign of those who know and are unified with the Law of the Hierarchy. Our rays are not granted to the lukewarm or to the hypocrites, but to those who truly love the light.

17. Magnificent vestments await beings in their new Dwelling!

18. Surrender of the ego is vital for the spirit to be liberated. The spirit cannot fly freely as long as it holds on to this disintegrating vortex on Earth. The higher will must absorb that which is below it. This is the law. This law is transporting humanity to new kingdoms beyond the dark swamp of free will.

19. You have correctly recognized the approach of Our Messenger. But greater detachment is needed. Ideas and expectations must be relinquished. All that you know must be put aside. You must be empty, not wanting anything. We know you deeply;

there is nothing that you can hide from Us. Keep your inner flame burning, since the Messenger will soon return.

20. Supremacy of the spirit over matter exists in potential but it needs to be awakened, activated and expanded. My Ray provides the beginning and the unfolding of this process. In this Ray the disciple finds strength to break down the obstacles along the path. You who have crossed the bridge of doubt and can advance firmly; do not lag behind. The new dawn awaits the bearers of its light.

21. Your triumphs mean nothing to the future that awaits you. Of what worth to you are the stepping stones left behind? They will be of use to those who come after you. This is also why one must go forward. The wayfarer walks through emptiness, for the spirit builds its path in the invisible. The new can only be perceived when it becomes manifested.

22. Great is the responsibility of those who follow the path, but even greater are the blessings they receive. The light of tomorrow reflects in the mirror of their hearts and thus spreads to the whole planet. Yes, each link of this chain of light is important to fulfill the task. Success depends not only on the power of the Source, which is boundless, but also on the determination and readiness of those who receive it. In these times, when dense fog hides the rays of the Sun, one must know how to discern. May the disciples not be discouraged when facing difficulties; but may they use their difficulties to whet the edge of their swords.

23. Heralds of a new dawn, you are the messengers of Light! Beneath your bare feet flows the stream of power and love which will renew the face of the planet. With your hands We are building the temple that will shelter the liberated spirit. In your hearts the robes of the new humanity are being woven with threads of eternity. Yes, We bless those who answer the Call. We strengthen the flow of the current of Good. We affirm the Supreme Will.

24. Whoever gets discouraged when attacked by the enemy is not ready to stand under the pure brilliance of light. As metal turns red when immersed in fire, so should the aura of those who seek the truth, incandesce. To journey in this planet the spirit must be a warrior and its decision to go forward must be firm. Its armor is forged in devotion to the Supreme Lord and the sign of the chosen shines on its forehead. Warrior of the Light, Our Peace sustains you!

25. The fire from space strengthens the ascending spirit. It is truly the breath and life of the spirit. May those who seek, come near. I will show them the way to the new Portal. Through attunement with the supreme will, what in the past took successive incarnations to be imprinted on matter, today is achieved in seconds. So fantasies and whims must be set aside. They are shadows that do not belong to the present.

26. Many students, when facing a new phase of the Teaching, look for proofs in the previous one. The essence is one. But only the seeds of the incoming phase can be found in the previous one. Students must turn within. There they will find all the proofs

needed.

27. If you recognized Me in the past, why would you not recognize Me now?

28. Do not let error become rooted in your heart. Pull it out right away and hand it over to Me. I accept it. I transform it into light. O, devoted disciple, you will know My Fire and in It I will transfigure you.

29. Continuous transformation of matter into light – this is how the path to subtleness unfolds. The planet is beginning to tread this path. A luminous future awaits it, a future that will reveal the key to contacting Our Council.

30. The evolutionary governance of the planet comes from the inner planes. Its true Hierarchy is composed of different levels of light. Humanity is being called to transcend the veils that hide these sublime realities and to cooperate in the manifestation of new times. This is why the existence of seven major centers was revealed to you and why Our Messengers so often draw near to you. The opportunity of these times is unique. Blessed be those who, though immersed in terrestrial darkness, believe in the light of dawn.

31. The Work is unending; its roots go deep into eternity. Each step taken becomes the basis for the next one and ongoing ascent vitalizes those who participate in it. Therefore, warn those who arrive – they must let themselves be permeated by the ardent fire

of supreme devotion; they must die to themselves; they must serve only one Lord. The sublime glory blesses those who thus surrender to the power of the spirit. In their flight they will reach the most distant Dwellings.

32. The flaming heart does not stop when facing difficulties in its ascent. It overcomes them all and thus becomes stronger. In them it glorifies the Lord. Like fragrance from a flower, gratitude emanates from the flaming heart. Its purity reflects the mysteries of the sky; its power redeems those who follow it. Blessed is the fire that consumes its existence and transports it to sublime levels! O, flaming heart, you have My Ray.

33. Ascent is built on the will. Therefore one must affirm the Good at every instant, not only in the nominal moments of prayer. These lands must be redeemed and cleansed of the disgrace of a dark past. May the disciple fuel the fire of Aurora,[1] which is now merging with its fellow centers.[2]

34. I do not lift all of the veils since the time has not yet come. You should follow the path step by step; in it you will find guidance and protection. I know every inch of this narrow path and I assure that I am with you. When darkness becomes even denser, remember: the light is near. Reaffirm your vows and go ahead. Do not give in to the allurements of the past; many depend upon your victory.

35. The power of the affirmation of the law is known by only

[1] Refers to the intraterrestrial center of Aurora.

[2] Refers to the other planetary centers active in the present stage of the Earth.

a few. The inertia of the world of matter must be decisively overcome. Penetrate this mystery, O disciple of truth! Affirm it! Build the fortress of the Good.

36. Before the end of this cycle, the planetary centers will be revealed even more openly. From them comes the pulsation that supports life on Earth.

37. There was a time when, in a special way, Aurora drew near to external life of the surface of the Earth. Some of its members even appeared in your cities and villages. We were preparing the aura of the planet for a wider manifestation of Our Brotherhood that was meant to occur in the present transition. Our program was reformulated. But this manifestation could still happen. The most important contact with Us, however, is the one established within the being and strengthened in fervor through transformation.

38. The centers vibrate in a new tone. Sharpen your hearing. Receive their splendor.

39. This chord is made up of many notes: three on seven, with four in its base and an infinity of sounds. How beautiful is the harmony that is ready to come forth. May the pure hearts be prepared, for the new Earth is being heralded. The Time of the Revelation is at hand.

40. You will come to know other centers on your spiritual journeys. In each one of them you will find a color and a sound; on each one you will leave your Name engraved in fire. Those

who tread the path of the Initiations know what I am talking about. Those who are preparing for it listen to these words and discover in their hearts the joy of what is to come. Seven doors open on different levels and twelve groups are waiting for their kin. It is time for rejoicing. The Encounter is at hand.

41. Why are you afraid? Why are you crying? You have only lost your prison bars! You have become free. Turn your face towards the dawn. Do not be disturbed by the doubts of mortals. In cruciform, spread open your arms and welcome the cross which is being given to you. Yes, your arms will become wings. Fly... the Infinite is your Dwelling.

42. Of what use are the promises of the little ones if they want what the law cannot give them? O, pain that consumes the flesh of these passers-by, how long will you be their teacher? Humankind chooses dark destinies. May light penetrate these spheres. Yes, the Light is near. Matter will be redeemed.

5. The Call – I

I speak to you in different languages. Thus, all of you may understand Me. There is no reason to veil the law. But you must be ready to fulfill it – if not, you will receive the Word but you will not hear it; you will see Me but not recognize Me. Listen to what I am telling you: the covenant has been prepared. Time will reveal it.

1. Seven winds blow through seven portals. Time foretells the end. How many will hear this call, that in the middle of the night, awakens those who are to follow it? The light of the stars was hidden, but it shines silently in the hearts of the elect. The path is narrow. You have My Hands. Receive the help. Call out. Are you ready to depart? You are no longer the same as before. The new seed is sprouting; it must grow.

2. There are seven keys; only one will open the door for you. There are twelve lights; only one will lead you. Receive this Mantle. You have fulfilled the task. Now you are to set out on a new journey.

3. Do not look for words to explain. Go deep into this stream – it is a bountiful source. Draw from this source; it is your breath of life. Sharpen your sword on the stone. The battle proceeds. Fellow beings are crying out for help. Before the end comes they must be rescued.

4. You have completed the tasks, but more will be given to you. Receive them with open hands. Sweat and blood will bless them. Death is certain. Life is reborn. O, life and light, life and light! You have been imprisoned but Time shortens time. All will be accomplished.

5. A fetid odor floods the face of the Earth. Forsaken bodies wander about in crowds. Brothers, how often have you been warned! But there is still time to act. Keep these words in your heart and in silence affirm the power of the law. Affirm the law. Depart.

6. The dark sun of the seven nights has already crossed the threshold. Now the light of the light will be reflected in the Great Mirror. The new dawn heralds the arrival of the human-gods, children of the Sun and the stars. Welcome, O bearers of peace!

7. Aurora announces the great light. The fire circulates through the spheres and sets aflame the clefts of lunar vibration. There is no past, no present, no future – only time. But time stopped. In the silence it scrutinizes the law. The law is fulfilled. It determines the exact position of each particle. Nothing remains where it was. Few are left. They are to follow on.

8. How can the winds bring new seeds if there is no ground to receive them? The earth has dried up. The rivers have dried up. Hunger spreads. The waters have been defiled. The pure streams have withdrawn and are now flowing inside the Earth. You know this. Aurora reveals the way. It is night, but do not halt your

journey, for you will have My light to guide you. Reach out to the ones who call for help. Do not be misled for there are those who lie, who do not want to proceed. Listen. Listen to My Voice within you. I have promised. I am with you. Go onward.

9. The spirit regenerates itself. The promise is kept. But once again humankind violates the law. Too late. Even the pure ones wallowed in the mud. They did not know how to persist. But there are those who keep on going. Two would be enough. But there are more than ten. These will reach the Portal. Sublime light awaits them. They bear the seal on their foreheads. It is the sign.

10. The past gives way to reality. Spirit transcends form. Form is demolished and light illuminates life. Aurora, your face and the faces of your brothers shine resplendently in the mirror of this universe. Today you are seven. As you know, tomorrow you will be more. The surface of the Earth will welcome you. Thus, it is written.

11. The children of the light have arrived. They know the way. They call each one on Earth by name, but not all respond. The little ones have gotten lost again. One cannot wait for them.

12. "What will tomorrow be like?" ask the thirsty humans. They are hungry… cold... lonely… but there is a path. How long will it take for the cycle to be accomplished? Seven nights, of

which three are already over. The time to come is not far off.

13. Do you want the truth? To receive it, your hands must be empty and your heart pure. The eyes of the soul will see the spirit. Resplendent face. The union is near, but this is not yet the time for it to happen. Go forward. Yours is the fire. Glorify it.

14. All the sayings of the world do not express even a syllable of the Word. The Word resounds – full of power! The power of the heavens opens up pathways, breaks down obstacles, and anchors the light. Repeat My Name. It is the portal. Go ahead, but barefooted. Fear not. Come close. Do not make comparisons. The Apostles also could not recognize their risen Master at first. Forget familiar standards. Delve into your heart. Open yourselves to the law. The time is for revelations.

15. The mysteries of the inner the Earth will be revealed to the pure. The mysteries of the depth of the seas will be revealed to the pure. The mysteries of the celestial heights will be revealed to the pure. But not all will see the face of the Archangel. Only three out of the nine touch the stream. They return, reborn. They have transcended death. They bring new laws. The others will proceed, risen. Three by three, in their own way. The laws are different for each level.

16. My Voice is the resounding of many voices. Those who have touched My fire recognize it. I foretell life. I bring you liberation. I am the One who comes and announces the One who comes. We are the Voice that should reverberate. I represent those

who merged into the light. They are on this Earth to rescue it. They are all in Me; I am in them. This is why you perceive new sounds from My tone. Go forward. Go forward. It is time to unveil new facets of this sacred universe which, through death, embraced the pain of those who were born in darkness.

17. Seven times, seven times seven, will I call. I speak to the world, but the world does not want the truth. It prefers the profusion of evil. The lost ones are even more lost. They fight among themselves. But I light up the portal. Those who love the Good must listen. Human justice is blind, but celestial justice sees and is wise. Celestial justice knows what it sees and what it does not see. Light approaches once again. Miracles happen. Peace reigns in the hearts of the pure, even if their bodies cannot keep on going. Night is a companion for it reveals universes to them; it brings them the message and keeps the secret. Come! Do not withhold your steps. This is a group speaking to you. Twelve groups are speaking to you. Love. You must go forward. The paths multiply beneath your feet. Many beings follow you, but you cannot see them. Go ahead! Affirm My Name. You have the sword. You have the law.

18. You hear choirs, not one voice only. It is My Voice revealing secrets to you. The sparks blaze. They are all One. There is no separation. The key unlatches the bolt to let evil out. It will not be eliminated all at once. But the fever will subside and the delirium will cease. Purify, purify this sick Earth. Healing is reborn. Come, Aurora, raise Your scepter. The task is Yours.

19. The one who knows, without having seen or heard, walks in faith. This is your path. Put aside the need for proof. Of what value is the past to the one who surrenders to eternity? The present hides the sacred pearl. Where is the diamond? In the center of the twelve. The Lord rises. The great star is on his forehead. Distant, but near. He rises. The twelve merge. The first one approaches.

20. I will reveal My Name. You know one of My Names, but not the one that is yet to come.

21. Sacred is the path that is being unveiled to humanity. It brings the keys to immortality. But do not be troubled with the weeping or with the cries of dread. The fires of the enemy will not touch those who have penetrated the secret of fire. There is still time but I say, the time is now. Regenerate the flesh where your spirit abides. Weave new, sacred robes with threads of light.

22. May those who can succeed go forth. May those who can love, give of themselves. Do not waste a single minute. The enemy stands guard, so be vigilant. We are twelve; above they are three and one. There are still others. O Devotion, lift up your sword and establish the law! The cosmos pleads. There is no pain yet pain does continue to exist on Earth. Come, O Great Light!

23. Those who were on the ferry did not dare. But one of them was saved. He was taken out. He knew the secret, the secret of light, and for this reason he worked in silence. He was a chosen one. And the others? They were called, but they did not

want to listen. Lightning. Storms. Wind. Pray in silence. The hour has come. Wait for the Messenger. Where is your faith?

24. Twelve flames blaze in My breast. Great is the heart. The One who comes needs a Portal. He already has it. He may approach.

25. The footprints on the ground do not set the path. The ground becomes transfigured; it is never the same. The path reappears in the kingdom of the spirit. New suns shine resplendently, spreading their light. The kaleidoscope turns, producing new forms. Its gems are also transformed.

26. The lilies weep for the innocent ones who were lost in the night. But they, too, will arrive. What was promised will be fulfilled. They will not see the light as will those who have persisted, but they will be led to a new dwelling, until they return to retrieve what they left behind.

27. The embers fade out if they find no sustainment. They must be fanned. Let the wind enter. It brings life. It kindles the flame in the heart of those who have forgotten it. There is still time. There will always be. But the pain is great and will have to be endured. New lights. The promise is fulfilled. Never before has there been such a great opportunity. Immense is the darkness. But the light will be still greater.

28. The elements, diverted by humanity, will have no one to obey. A destructive mechanism has engendered the sin of the

ages. The past repeats itself. Once more the suffering of the world is excruciating. But it will not be as before. The door has opened and nevermore will it close. The stars draw near. They were hidden; now they are revealing themselves. They chant canticles foretelling the Coming.

29. Devoted offering, you are made of silver; I will transform you into light. Lay at My feet whatever impurity you may have. Lay at My feet the most sacred things you may bring. My Mantle is an unfolding of the Mantle of the Lord. In it I gather your clamor and your gifts. It is made of fire. It transforms everything. It redeems everything. It transmutes everything. Yes, you have recognized My Name and you are Blessed. The stars know this.

30. You can sew with one needle, but with two you can weave a mantle – you will know the secret of the polarities.

31. Seven colors emanate from the center. Another five remain above. From the second emerges the first. The third is born. The one is enriched. The three ascend, on four, on seven. The colors dwindle, only one shines. All of them must return to the center; they cannot bring back what departed. The first shines resplendently. The colors come forth. Now they are twelve. A level higher. Unity is revealed. The second merges into the first. It must depart again.

32. Further information will be transmitted to you. However, the time has not yet come. The rope must be stretched to breaking point. Many have already gone. Others will still go. However, an enormous throng remains. It has joined up with evil. It has

refused the light. May those who waver receive the strike of the law on their faces. There is still time. May they awaken. May they proceed. May they love.

33. Even louder will the innocent call out for help. They are pure. They were deluded by earthly rulers. They plead; their faith is true. Their cries will be heard and they will not be forgotten. They never will be. They will know paradise on Earth. They will have to work for it. But they have chosen it so. They are generous. They belong to the Good.

34. Not only two, but three saints remain. They work in silence. They know peace, as well as strife. They are devoted. Faithful lovers of the law. They serve night and day. The light approaches and can be anchored in them. They have opened the door to it. The light comes closer and uplifts the pure ones. The sky lights up. They know My Mantle. My Voice resounds in them.

35. Those who depart leave unbeknown. Those who know, say nothing. They pray in silence. They pray, and thus they serve. It is necessary to pray. More departures, always in silence. The contact has taken place. The hour is at hand. The Messenger goes forth. He knows all the doors and has the key to each one. He asks for the password. Few are able to respond. He gathers the chosen ones. They have been sealed for all time. And the others? They heard but believed not what they had heard.

36. The scorching sun will not burn you. The iciness of the night will not freeze you. Hunger will not torment you. Keep

going forward; you have Me. The universe is My being.

37. The day darkened. Humans did not perceive it. The waters became murky. Humans kept up their furtive practices. The ground opened up into fissures and humans tried to cover them with new errors. Too late. But there is time for those who transcend darkness. They were sealed before descending. They knew what lay ahead, nevertheless they forgot where they had come from. This was also envisioned. And life is transformed. Such is the law. There is still a distance to cover. Be vigilant. Not in fear, which is the cradle of cowards, nor in flight, which is the pathway of liars, but rather in forgiveness will you become uplifted. If you want to serve, you have My Mantle. You have My sword. Bow before the law. Seven nights, one still missing. Be not dismayed!

38. A dense darkness formed in those whereabouts. It was nurtured by human will. However, some sought the light and persevered. They suffered, but learned their lessons. They went down, but wanted to climb up. They got lost, but found their way again. They are not many, but their clamor spanned universes. This was sufficient. The pain went on and will still go on, but it will not outlast tomorrow.

39. Thirteen are enough to make up the arc. There are more than thirteen. It is finished. Twelve must depart. One remains. But the twelve are within it. The new cycle begins.

40. Sacred pearls were cast into the mire. But they were not

lost. Nor were they blemished. They will regain their luster when the rains wash the soil and the wind cleans the air. They are twelve. They were safeguarded. They remained hidden.

41. Twenty-one flames blaze in the Lord's crown. Seven, seven and seven. They expand and open the portal. The warriors arriving from afar are welcomed. They have come to save. Priests, come forward in silence. Healers, you have your fields to harvest. Many come to help. They are legion. They will leave when the task is finished. But great is the labor. Aurora, take Your stand. Yours is the reconstruction.

42. The sounds have died down. Silence permeates everything. But transformation goes on, intense, deep. Step by step, particle by particle. The law is reborn. My being rejoices. May the faithful return. To them I offer Paradise.

6. The Call – II

The night was imprisoned. But now it has been set free. It keeps vigil for the coming of the Brothers. Blessed are those who know the secrets it harbors. They heard about the law and wanted to follow it. Imperfect, they sought perfection.

1. A failing can be fatal. The tension is great. But he knows the secret. He controls matter. He overcame the trials. He crossed the threshold. His eyes bear the radiance of My Ray. We are one. But he must watch out. The enemies dress in white and try to dissuade him from the goal. However, they destroy that which they themselves built.

2. The bodies can no longer restrain the pressure of the fire which, from within, turns outward and intensifies. It is the fire of life; through death it consumes the matter that is meant to survive. In the past, this circuit had to be repeated seven times. Now, only three. The truth has been revealed to you. Be not afraid of what is new. Much is still to come.

3. You recognize My Sound by its vibrations in your centers. Shake off the dust of the past. May those who want to repeat patterns go back to the dead letter. You knew well the importance of the dates on which the information was transmitted to you. For everything a cycle, for every cycle a law. Renewal is relent-

less. Time is no longer what you think it is. The spheres merge; redemption has begun. Great will be the glory and you will be able to experience it. Put aside that which is no longer of any use to you. Raise your consciousness fervently. Go forward. Everything is stipulated. It has been written. It will be fulfilled.

4. Seek the truth within life. Leave the need for proof to the unbelievers. They will have their proofs. But they will not be able to know My Name. Blessed are those who contact the essence. Blessed are those who embrace its rays in silence. The spheres vibrate; they echo new conjunctures. Very powerful sounds issue forth from the cosmos. Look at the constellations. They harbor secrets. You will penetrate all of them, one by one. Cross the portal. My Ray summons you. It is time to depart.

5. Nine over twelve. The three are uplifted. Three, and then six. Such must be the progression. But do not be rigid. They were seven, now twelve live and vibrate the new tone. Glory, infinite is the glory of the new existence. It already exists. It has always existed. But it was hidden. Now it is revealing itself. Another veil falls away. Proceed. One must be careful. One must be prudent. One must have courage. Press on.

6. Only one will remain. All are this one; it is in them all. This is why boundaries slip through the fingers of those who attempt to analyze. The new time has begun. You are already living it. Tune your instrument. You will have to sound new chords. The spirit – freed. The Earth, once shiftless, is now reborn, full of light and power.

7. All journey on. All of them. Forwards or backwards. The spheres move, one over the other. The stars move – everything has changed. Do not look for reference points, you will not find them. Pray. Do not pay attention to rumors. They are false. You will know Truth within you. How can you recognize the Messenger? You will know the Truth within you. How not to be misled? Have faith.

8. What remained is taken away. The beginning is underway. Aurora knows no rest. It works – night and day, night and day. On each plane, in each sphere, night and day. Angelic hosts assist it in the task. Terrestrial humans cannot take part in this work. New designs emerge. On each plane, in each sphere. New threads, new patterns. The angels give praise. They know what reverence is. They fulfill the law. They love, they do not doubt. Phalanx of the Sound, they weave the patterns of the new life.

9. Three on three. Thus the new weaving enlarges. The seeds were sown in the past. Now they are sprouting. Three on three. The essence is one. It has always been present. New forms, new sounds. More perfect, more beautiful, more subtle. The density has vanished. The prophets knew that this would happen and they said so. But the past is far away. However – not timewise, because time has also changed.

10. The cloud of death has been exterminated. Evil has been turned into good. Everything has always been under control. But the battle was necessary. Now peace reigns. The journey goes on. Always upwards.

11. Those who once were great among men now belong to the Sun or to what lies beyond it. The Voice of the centers resounds. The centers are mirrors which reflect the face of the new life. They embrace the new life. They are one. The innocent, who left, come back purified. A new phase of building begins. Aurora hands over its role. There are other Brothers.

12. The three endure. They are three and they are one. But the feminine principle rules. O City of the Sun, your towers rise up above the Earth; you can already be seen by the Brothers. You are blessed. You know the secret. There will always be a secret.

13. Twelve proceed onward. They are the very dawn. Their light is the light of tomorrow as well as the light of today and yesterday. It is eternal, unchangeable. Total, it is revealed in phases that call for human participation. This is why it has waited to dawn. Now the final moment has come; it is just the beginning.

14. You try to compare what you have now received to what you already know. In this way you will be confused. Within yourself you will know who speaks to you. It is I. My light is the Light of the World. My key opens all the doors of this universe, from the first to the last. The Councils speak to you. They speak through My Voice. Be aware that there are not two, but one. Unity reigns throughout the higher spheres where there is no division. But listen to the crying of the simple. They want to become free. Go forth and rescue them.

15. The nine who stayed will reveal themselves. The other three will rise and merge into the Sun. Yes, this universe expands, widening its boundaries. The Earth will live new laws and so will its companion planets. Look at the stars. O, so many secrets! But you will recognize the Portal. Cross it and be blessed. You will be in peace.

16. Distant worlds approach the Earth. It is redemption. Three suns are one; the regent also ascends. The purification goes on, but you must not control it. The laws of transmutation work in silence. They act. They deal with energy. Welcome to You, Brothers, Who are always arriving! Others depart. They have fulfilled their tasks. Everyone prepares for the coming of the Great One. He will come.

17. Nights contemplating Infinity. The dawn reveals secrets. The visitors approach in silence. They call those who must depart, always in silence. They leave no signs. But this is the sign. Those who are aware, know this, but they do not know the hour.

18. The flesh has become corrupt; it opens up into wounds. The Earth also weeps. It grieves the suffering of its children. But all will pass. Have faith. It is necessary to cleanse this Dwelling. Everything is under control. Look up – you will recognize Us. We are with you. Await your time. Have faith.

19. There are neither governments nor governors. Chaos reigns. This is the scene of the surface of life. We had warned you that this would happen. But there are other realities. Some of you know them.

20. Lights across the skies. Now, during the day. Redeeming lights. They are cherished by some and hated by others. Evil has not yet ended. But the time is near when it will happen. The cycles must be accomplished.

21. The winds uncover what has been hidden by lies. They move the desert sands, exposing what was beneath. But the cloud increases, corrodes and degrades. Where to go? Pray.

22. Stagnation gives off a putrid odor. Many drink of it. They have become used to it. But there are those who walk silently towards the mountains. The places are marked. They have always been. We have announced it so many times! The planet was in danger of succumbing, but now it is safe. However, the operation has not ended. Humanity is still in danger.

23. Hundreds, thousands, millions. Hoards of famished as far as the eye can see. They did not know how to recognize the signs. Now, they suffer for the past. But the future will not be long. Everything will be transformed.

24. The spheres expand. It is the new law. The spheres merge. You are living future times. But it is not you who are living them, because the spirit has become free. Know that, for eons, stars have kept watch over the Earth. Now it is free.

25. In the fields the seeds begin to germinate. Gratitude has not died. The springs, once withdrawn, now flow again. Their waters descended to the depths and returned purified, bringing

new tunes. The angels know this. Angels of light, angels of sound, angels of the ethers. The Brotherhood is present. The Councils, five of them, can go into action. The new unsown field is being seeded. But it is necessary to strengthen what emerges. So proclaims the Sun.

26. Groups are formed. How distant the past has become, and yet, how near it is! What was on High regenerated what was below. But one must keep on going. May humans know how to recognize it. They will know.

27. Flowers begin to bloom. Beauty is incorruptible. Its seeds, eternal. They drift in the wind. The birds carry them, in silence. There is joy in the air. A new beginning.

28. Humans sold what did not belong to them. They made the same mistakes as their ancestors. Greed hardened their heart. So many ailments! So much suffering! But there is no lack of forgiveness for those who know how to seek it. Tears will dry up. May the chosen ones come. May those who love, come. Purity will be achieved during the journey. It is miraculous. It is eternal. It was already there, but veiled. Now there is no way to hide it. Let the light shine. New universe. Your Face, O Lord.

29. Many are taken away. They do not have to be a part of the ending. Others stay on to serve. But the spheres interpenetrate. Great is the help. Miracles. Yes, miracles do happen to those who have faith. The energy of miracles had to be imprinted on the material sphere. The day has dawned. Aurora blesses it.

30. The sacred flames come up on the horizon. They are twelve. They merge into the Great Sun. They emanated from it and now return to it. They still do not manifest perfection, but they are becoming united. Perfection is their goal. It shall be accomplished.

31. Nine times three. Humanity moves on. The cycles set the pace. Harmony is there, albeit still underway. Space is no longer the same. Its laws have changed. The corrosive rains have long been gone. They are not needed any more. All is calm. But one must move forward. The turning of the cycles ordains it. The Councils approach; they bring the laws. Now humans want to listen to them. They have learned. They have been purified.

32. Space evolves. It has its own existence. It does not depend on humans, but it encompasses and interacts with them. It encompasses the stars. It is one, but is composed of many – one inside the other. Its Regents unfold, but they emanate from the One. They also seek perfection. The whole universe ascends. The journey is infinite. The Regents know this. They love it. They are the children of love.

33. Those who have crossed the threshold of the spiritual kingdom no longer need the concept of time. Beings have their existence on several levels; their evolution is not chronological. In each sphere they respond differently to the impulses from the Councils. Fire from space is necessary because it draws the particles together and leads them toward the ascent. Venus knows it. It was taught this by the Sun.

34. Consciousness crosses into eternity. It becomes deluded with the succession of events. But all of the events are present at the same time. They come to light, one after the other. What is time? It has also changed.

35. The space vessels become manifest. The Brotherhood in action. It is the fulfillment of the promise. It is redemption. The space vessels are made of light. They move the ethers, performing miracles. Humans watch them. Not all surrender to the law. But those who do, discover love.

36. Flame of devotion, permeate your children. Flame of power, teach them the law. Flame of love, you belong to all.

37. There are many pathways, but only one leads humanity to its final destination. I speak of ultimate destiny, the great consummation. But it remains distant in time. It is the goal; everyone journeys towards it.

38. How unconscious humans are! They perpetuate error and sin. The cosmos clamors for harmony. But they do not want to listen to it. The earth is shattered. Humanity was warned. Justice has to be carried out. The spheres can only ascend if humanity settles its debts.

39. Humanity is one. It belongs to the cosmos. It dwells in the cosmos. It penetrates different spheres; it approaches the Creator. I refer to the Life that nourishes life in humankind. But the humans of this Earth tried to separate themselves from Life. They

attempted, but they did not succeed. They destroyed the form, but not the sacred current. The cycles are being fulfilled.

40. Nine laws are the most important. Three are the main ones. You will receive them one by one and you must fulfill them. They express the new patterns. They bring new ethics, which take into account the liberated beings and their relationship with the cosmos. Listen to the One who speaks to you inwardly.

41. Those who yearn for the spirit will be blessed. Those who seek their sustenance in matter will have to go on looking for it in matter. Do not deceive yourselves, or your brothers. Those who surrender to the Most High die to themselves. This is the only way they are reborn into the light. This is the destiny of the pure. They were not afraid of death. They transcended it. They knew Life. They merged into It.

42. Do not be proud of your achievements. The breach is about to happen. Strong arms and ardent hearts will be needed. Servers who recognize the Word and know how to enunciate It.

7. The Call – III

The fire that is immanent in the universe expands. The channels widen and facilitate the circulation of the fire of space. Permeated by this fire, consciousness increases its receptivity. The mold also becomes luminous. The radiance of light increases. In the pause between one breath and another, the fusion of the spheres occurs. The essence is set free and ascends to a new level.

1. Worlds in different dimensions interconnect through invisible channels. The same happens with human subtle bodies. Before, they were apart; now the dividing veils are being dissolved.

2. Light-consciousness awakens. In each cell, in each being. This is the work of Aurora. You have been told. Partake in it.

3. The pathway of fire in space may be expressed mathematically. But not with terrestrial knowledge. The movement of this fire expands the Consciousness in the Rulers and in the particles of the universes. Each Ruler has a specific numerical combination, which designates its Ray and field of action. Sound can also be expressed by mathematical interrelationships. Be attentive to the symbols We transmit to you.

4. Each planet is a universe or part of a universe. Councils govern the relationship among universes. The Councils are part of more powerful dynamos. You cannot fathom the totality of this circuit. Nevertheless, pursue this ascent.

5. Space encompasses myriads of lives. Many are in a dormant state, awaiting the time to become active. Humans do not realize the imbalance they cause by what they constantly send into space. Intense and continuous work is needed to protect these lives. May the servers heed their thoughts.

6. Space is pervaded by consciousness. Form shelters consciousness. The universes are consciousness in movement. My Ray has been there from the beginning and is present again at each new stage. Yet it is never absent. It is in the origin, throughout the course, and in the final consummation. I speak of this universe. There are others where I am also present.

7. Consciousness is your field of work. Whether you touch a grain of sand – or reach out to the infinite cosmos – you are contacting consciousness. Be not deluded by appearances.

8. Plenitude is a quality of the liberated consciousness. Plenitude fills the cosmos. Plenitude is the consecration of silence. Manifestation is present in the core of the Immutable. To merge into this reality, one must ascend step by step.

9. Myriads and myriads of particles... O infinite universe! It has its sphere of action. The beginning and the end are always there. If you seek to grasp this reality, transcend the illusion of form and contact the essence.

10. The inter-relationship between the primordial impulse of expansion and the final impulse of absorption into the ori-

gin gives rise to the cycles of universal existence. The cycles are appearances – consciousness in action.

11. Three phases of the fire. Expressions of the essence in different gradations. They are halos around the one flame of existence. Fire is life. Fire vivifies the particles of the cosmic universe. Fire is the life-breath of the Great Builder. Fire is the face of the non-manifested life-impulse. Fire veils your Name. Fire is your pathway. Fire transmutes your being. Fire is Our language. Fire enkindles the Word. Fire knows the secret of the manifested Word.

12. Beyond the range of the Hierarchies of this planetary universe, distant galaxies watch over the evolution of life in this galaxy and this solar system. Echoes of this process powerfully transform planetary spheres.

13. Consciousness is present in each and every particle. It vibrates in all of them. It seeks to expand. The human kingdom is a delicate link in the evolutionary chain. In it, life awakens to self-existence. But consciousness is infinite. Life is infinite. Power is the will-impulse of life. Power is the propelling force of the universes. Consciousness is liberated through power.

14. Ever since the beginning of the present cycle of manifestation of this system, a link has been established between this solar system and the Central Government of the Cosmos, as well as certain galaxies representing it. Jupiter safeguards the secret of this inter-connection.

15. Infinite are the potentialities of manifested life. But little of this is known to humans because they have limited themselves to the primary laws of evolution in matter. Through supraphysical sidereal engineering, the cosmic Brotherhood set up work bases which, to humans, appear to be planets.

16. A planet that does not belong to this solar system rotates far away around this Sun. The Regency of the planet, and not its trajectory in space, determines the solar system to which it belongs.

17. A well known planet of this solar system is actually an inter-galactic base – an artificial satellite built within the laws of supra-consciousness.

18. Humans are deluded by their external senses. They have forgotten the presence of worlds in different dimensions. If they only knew what a sublime existence the Sun is! And how insignificant they are before the splendor of life on other stars...

19. You can see that we are presenting different subjects. All of them are to help you transcend the human level and to call you to the mysteries of Creation by different routes. It must be so. Our seeds are to reach and to sprout in those who are attuned and receptive. Welcome to the daring, to the brave, to those who do not fear death, who love life and who give themselves totally to it.

20. Mars awaits in silence. But its essence ascends rapidly.

21. The present transition is not limited to this planetary universe; it embraces the entire galaxy. Therefore, put aside what is known and prepare for higher flights.

22. The disintegration of the physical body of the Moon will be speeded up. It will disappear but an inter-systemic base will be installed in the orbit of the Earth. Sirius knows this.

23. Once again the seven sisters seek another quadrant. They remain linked with this universe, but in a new attunement.

24. The human mind cannot apprehend cosmic existence. We are giving you impulses for your ascent. Do not turn them into museum pieces.

25. The seven sisters summon this humanity. The Archer prepares his bow of light to shoot anew. Before the portal closes, all that is possible must be done for this parched soil and for the suffering beings who tread it. In essence, this Teaching contains the wisdom of the past. One step in the ascent. The fire will not be found in the layers of dust on the books, but in the hearts of the pilgrims. May they learn to go forward.

26. Orion will reveal its key to the Earth. Saturn has received it.

27. Cosmic combinations... What a beautiful symphony! These sublime chords will finally be able to penetrate the Earth-

universe.

28. Chanting a soft melody, Lyra takes up its new position. It will find three apexes in this solar system to support it.

29. The dragon persists. Rooting out evil is a gradual process. But everything is under control. Can you see the face of the Silent Watcher?

30. Journeys among galaxies go on continuously. To understand them you must let go of your materialistic concepts of time and space. Remember that the manifested universe is consciousness in movement. So, where are the boundaries?

31. The consciousness-light in you has to be awakened if you are to glimpse the reality of Our space vessels. When human beings dream while sleeping, where are the environments and people they contact? "Within their own consciousness," you will say. Therefore, I ask you: "and when they are awake?" I tell you that there is no difference between these states, except in vibration. The entire cosmos is consciousness. So, Our space vessels are also consciousness. They are the full expression of light-consciousness. They transcend material laws and may have total control over the sphere where they operate. Do not be deluded by the materialness that you perceive in the universe through your senses.

32. The present civilization has used physical matter for its constructions. It based itself on the densest and most rudimenta-

ry aspect of the fire of space and its most primary laws. Processed through friction, such slow procedures generate waste and energy-loss. Humanity of the future will be given knowledge of the higher aspects of fire. Thus the new Earth will utilize different means.

33. What is the universe but a thought? Enter into this mystery, so often expressed and so little assimilated by humankind.

34. Seven lights shine from the body of the Great Bear. Five emanate from its center. Draw near. You will realize that reality is much greater.

35. The science of numbers will arise anew in the coming Earth. Now it is merely obscure manipulation by wizards. In the future it will become luminous knowledge revealed in symbols for humanity to unveil the Thought of the Cosmos.

36. Those who let themselves be transfigured into light reach the Source of Power. They become bearers of the celestial fire. This Source exists deep inside each particle. Therefore, matter must not be profaned. Humans lost their link with the cosmos, but they are about to recover it. May they respond to this call in time.

37. May what will happen on the surface of the planet not disturb you. Humans have become used to chronic evil and are astounded when they notice the tumor they themselves have generated. Raise your consciousness and be heralds of light. You

have a reason to be incarnated. Do not betray your own destiny. Great is the loss when a messenger strays from the designated path and fails to fulfill the task. Therefore, be on guard... be on guard. Do not give in to evil. Life – not decay – is your destiny.

38. Vestiges of the past do not sidetrack those who are truly united to the Hierarchy. They hold no other remembrance in their hearts but their cosmic origins, to which they will return.

39. All particles will one day return to the Source. But today servers of the light must urgently engage in right action in the sphere of matter. I tell you, do not delay your decision: dedicate yourself to nothing else but your task. Service should be foremost in your life and in the life of the planet. Many say they cannot serve on account of karmic ties. They are mistaken. That service is precisely what would balance out their karmic debts and raise them to higher levels. These are not normal times. You are on the threshold of a new actuality. Therefore, a split second may be worth an entire existence. Discern wisely and dedicate yourself wholeheartedly.

40. We must warn you to the very last moment: be watchful. Evil never gives up. Even when overcome, it leaves chaos behind. Therefore, burn the laurels of victory in the fire of your heart as an offering to the Most High. Hasten, wayfarer, and firmly ward off the enemy.

41. Hold in silence what we will tell you in secret. Keep Our Messages in your heart. Refine your attunement. The inner light

must shine into the outer world. Inner sound must echo through the ethers of this universe. May the boundaries between the inner and the outer be dissolved. Put aside all prejudice. Make no comparisons. You are at a threshold. Follow the outpouring from your inner self. Time does not exist. Remember: all is consciousness. Where are the One who instructs and the one who is instructed?

42. The sound of distant universes reaches you and awakens light-consciousness. Listen to My Voice. It is the Voice of the universes. It points to the path to be followed. It summons you to the cries of those who are in need. My Voice calls you to service and reveals the light to you.

Enter the Flame. The time is now.
You have My blessing.

Amhaj

About Trigueirinho and His Work

Jose Trigueirinho Netto (1931-2018) was born in Sao Paulo, Brazil. He lived in Europe for a number of years, where he maintained contact with individuals who were advanced on the spiritual path, including Paul Brunton.

In his own life he was an example of the teachings that he transmitted through his books and talks about the transcendence and elevation of the human being, the contact with the soul and with even more profound nuclei of the being, impersonal service, and the link with the Spiritual Hierarchies.

One of the fundamental elements of his work is to stimulate the expansion of human consciousness and to liberate it from the bonds that keep it imprisoned to material aspects of existence, both external and internal.

He was the Founder of the Community of Light Figueira (http://www.comunidadefigueira.org.br) and a Founder and member of the Board of Directors of the Fraternity International

Humanitarian Federation (www.fraterinternacional) as well as a Co-Founder of the Grace Mercy Order, an ecumenical Christian monastic order. He also was an active collaborator, instructor and spiritual protector of three other communities located in Uruguay, Argentina and Portugal.

In his last 30 years he lived in the Community of Light Figueira, in the interior of Minas Gerais, Brazil, a community that at present has approximately 300 residents and which is visited annually by thousands of collaborators who are members of a larger network of humanitarian services and of spiritual studies that was always guided and followed closely by Trigueirinho.

Thanks to his inestimable instruction and his love for the Kingdoms of Nature and as a result of the exemplary work that he himself implanted in the Figueira community, the Animal, Vegetable and Mineral Kingdoms are the recipients of loving treatment there.

Trigueirinho wrote over 80 books, published originally in Portuguese, with many of them translated into Spanish, English, French and German. He gave more than 3,000 talks that were recorded live and which are available in CD, with some available in DVD and pen drive. Approximately 100 of these recorded talks are available with English voice over at the website of the Shasti Association: http://www.shasti.org/instruction (drop down the menu tab titled "Trigueirinho Instruction" and then click on "MP3 audios").

The primary focus of the first phase of Trigueirinho's work was concerned with self-knowledge, prayer, instruction and spiritual transformation. Following this, he began to transmit information with respect to Universal Life and about the assistance that humanity has from its beginnings received by means of the Intra-terrestrial White Brotherhood which inhabits the Retreats and the Planetary Centers as well as through the Cosmic Brotherhood of the Universe. He provides information about the presence of the Spiritual Hierarchy on the planet and the advent of the new humanity.

His work also includes themes relating to: the need for humanity to balance the negative karmas that it has created in relation to the Kingdoms of Nature; the negative karmic burden that we carry from the history of slavery and the genocide of indigenous peoples; and the nature of spiritual work in groups. He also addresses issues of healing, a larger vision of astrology, the esoteric nature of symbols, sound and colors, and the divine feminine.

In his last eight years he analyzed with clarity and with the wisdom that always characterized him, the messages that the Divinity has been giving to the planet as a warning to humanity (available from www.mensajerosdivinos.org/en).

His work reveals a real comprehension of the significance of all the Kingdoms of Nature on our planet, the true spiritual task of the human being, its place in the universe and also its responsibility before Creation.

Finally, he clarifies the reasons for the crisis that today is devastating humanity, teaching how to avoid reacting negatively to an immanent natural catastrophe by contacting more subtle levels of consciousness, and opening perspectives for the beginning of a more luminous cycle for our race.

Books by Trigueirinho

(Books available in English have English title first)

Published by Editora Pensamento
Sao Paulo, Brazil

1987

Nossa Vida Nos Sonhos
OUR LIFE IN DREAMS

A Energia Dos Raios Em Nossa Vida
THE ENERGY OF THE RAYS IN OUR LIVES

1988

Do Irreal Ao Real
FROM THE UNREAL TO THE REAL

Hora de Crescer Interiormente
O Mito de Hércules Hoje
TIME FOR INNER GROWTH – *The Myth of Hercules Today*

A Morte Sem Medo e Sem Culpa
DEATH WITHOUT FEAR AND WITHOUT GUILT

Caminhos Para a Cura Interior

PATHS TO INNER HEALING

1989

ERKS – *Mundo Interno*

ERKS – *The Inner World*

Miz Tli Tlan – *Um Mundo que Desperta*

MIZ TLI TLAN – *A World that Awakens*

Aurora – Essência Cósmica Curadora

AURORA – *Cosmic Essence of Healing*

Signs of Contact

SINAIS DE CONTATO

O Novo Começo do Mundo

THE NEW BEGINNING OF THE WORLD

A Quinta Raça

THE FIFTH RACE

Padrões de conduta para a nova Humanidade

PATTERNS OF CONDUCT FOR THE NEW HUMANITY

Novos Sinais de Contato

NEW SIGNS OF CONTACT

Os Jardineiros do Espaço

THE SPACE GARDENERS

1990

A Busca da Síntese

THE SEARCH FOR SYNTHESIS

Noah's Vessel

A NAVE DE NOÉ

Tempo de Retiro e Tempo de Vigília
A TIME OF RETREAT AND A TIME OF VIGIL

1991

Portas do Cosmos
GATEWAYS OF THE COSMOS

Encontro Interno – *A Consciência-Nave*
INNER ENCOUNTER – *The Consciousness Space Vessel*

A Hora do Resgate
THE TIME OF RESCUE

O Livro Dos Sinais
THE BOOK OF SIGNS

Mirna Jad – *Santuário Interior*
MIRNA JAD – *Inner Sanctuary*

As Chaves de Ouro
THE GOLDEN KEYS

1992

Das Lutas à Paz
FROM STRUGGLE TO PEACE

A Morada Dos Elisíos THE ELYSIAN DWELLING PLACE

Hora de Curar – *A Existência Oculta*
TIME FOR HEALING – *The Occult Existence*

O Ressurgimento de Fátima Lis
THE RESURGENCE OF FATIMA LIS

História Escrita nos Espelhos

Princípios de Comunicação Cósmic

HISTORY WRITTEN IN THE MIRRORS -

Principles of Cosmic Communication

Passos Atuais

STEPS FOR NOW

Viagem por Mundos Sutis

TRAVEL THROUGH SUBTLE WORLDS

Segredos Desvelados – *Iberah e Anu Tea*

UNVEILED SECRETS – *Iberah and Anu Tea*

A Criação – *Nos Caminhos da Energia*

CREATION – *On the Paths of Energy*

The Mystery of the Cross In the Present Planetary Transition

O MISTÉRIO DA CRUZ NA ATUAL TRANSIÇÃO PLANETÁRIA

O Nascimento da Humanidade Futura

THE BIRTH OF THE FUTURE HUMANITY

1993

Aos Que Despertam

TO THOSE WHO AWAKEN

Paz Interna em Tempos Críticos

INNER PEACE IN CRITICAL TIMES

A Formação de Curadores

THE FORMATION OF HEALERS

Profecias aos Que Não Temem Dizer Sim

PROPHECIES FOR THOSE WHO ARE NOT AFRAID TO SAY YES

The Voice of Amhaj

A VOZ DE AMHAJ

O Visitante – O Caminho Para Anu Tea

THE VISITOR –*The Way to Anu Tea*

A Cura da Humanidade

THE HEALING OF HUMANITY

Os Números e a Vidas – *Uma Nova Compreensão da Simbologia Oculta nos Números*

NUMBERS AND LIFE – *A New Understanding of Occult Symbolism in Numbers*

Niskalkat – *Uma Mensagem para os Tempos de Emergência*

NISKALKAT – *A Message for Times of Emergency*

Encontros Com a Paz

ENCOUNTERS WITH PEACE

Novos Oráculos

NEW ORACLES

Um Novo Impulso Astrológico

A NEW ASTROLOGICAL IMPULSE

1994

Bases do Mundo Ardente – *Indicações para Contato com os Mundos suprafíscicos*

BASES OF THE FIERY WORLD – *Indications for Contacts with Supraphysical Worlds*

Contatos com um Monastério Interaterreno

CONTACTS WITH AN INTRATERRESTRIAL MONASTERY

Os oceanos têm Ouvidos
OCEANS HAVE EARS

A Trajetória do Fogo
THE PATH OF FIRE

Glossário Esotérico
ESOTERIC LEXICON

1995

The Light Within You
A LUZ DENTRO DE TI

1996

Doorway to a Kingdom
PORTAL PARA UM REINO

Beyond Karma
ALÉM DO CARMA

1997

We Are Not Alone
NÃO ESTAMOS SÓS

Winds of the spirit
VENTOS DO ESPÍRITO

Finding the Temple
O ENCONTRO DO TEMPLO

There is Peace
A PAZ EXISTE

1998

Path Without Shadows

CAMINHO SEM SOMBRAS

Mensagens para Uma Vida de Harmonia

MESSAGES FOR A LIFE OF HARMONY

1999

Toque Divino

THE DIVINE TOUCH

Coleçào Pedaços de Céu

BITS FROM HEAVEN COLLECTION

- **Aromas do Espaço**
  AROMAS FROM SPACE
- **Nova Vida Bate à Porta**
  A NEW LIFE AWAITS YOU
- **Mais Luz No Horizonte**
  MORE LIGHT ON THE HORIZON
- **O Campanário Cósmico**
  THE COSMIC CAMPANILE
- **Nada Nos Falta**
  WE LACK NOTHING
- **Sagrados Mistérios**
  SACRED MYSTERIES
- **Ilhas de Salvaçáo**
  ISLANDS OF SALVATION

2002

Calling Humanity

UM CHAMADO ESPECIAL

2004

És Viajante Cósmico
YOU ARE A COSMIC WAYFARER

Impulsos
IMPULSES

2005

Pensamentos para Todo o Ano
THOUGHTS FOR THE WHOLE YEAR

2006

Trabalho Espiritual com a Mente
SPIRITUAL WORK WITH THE MIND

Published by Editora Irdin
Carmo da Cachoeira, Minas Gerais, Brazil

2009

Signs of Blavatsky – *An Unusual Encounter for the Present Time*
SINAIS DE BLAVATSKY – *Um Inusitado Encontro nos Dias de Hoje*

2012

Consciências e Hierarquias
CONSCIOUSNESSES AND HIERARCHIES

2015

Mensagens Reunidas

COLLECTED MESSAGES

Mensagens para Sua Tranformaçã

MESSAGES FOR YOUR TRANSFORMATION

2017

Páginas de Amor e Compreensão

PAGES OF LOVE AND COMPREHENSION

2018

Novos Tempos: Nova Postura

NEW TIMES: NEW ATTITUDE

2020

Versos Livres

OBRA PÓSTUMA

Trigueirinho's works are published by:

Associação Irdin Editora – www.irdin.org.br (selected titles of books in English, Spanish and Portuguese and CDs in several languages), Carmo da Cachoeira, MG, Brazil.

Editora Pensamento – www.pensamento-cultrix.com.br (titles in Portuguese), São Paulo, SP, Brazil

Editorial Kier – www.kier.com.ar (selected titles in Spanish), Buenos Aires, Argentina.

Lichtwelle-Verlag – www.lichtwelle-verlag.ch (selected titles in Spanish and German), Zurich, Switzerland.

Shasti Association – www.shasti.org (selected titles in English), Mount Shasta, CA, USA

Lectures of Trigueirinho with Simultaneous English Translation

During over thirty years as Founder of the Figueira Community of Light, Trigueirinho gave bi-weekly lectures (called 'parthilha's or 'sharings') that were recorded live. Audience members were invited to submit questions to him which were placed in a small box and brought to him by an attendant. Arriving early, Trigueirinho sat at the lectern, reading through and taking notes on the audience questions. Thus, his lectures often began with the phrase "someone has asked a question…." After addressing some of these questions, he continued with the theme chosen for the day.

Approximately 70 of these 'sharings' were later dubbed with English translations. His voice or the translators can be augmented or diminished by adjusting the right-left balance of the recording.

To access these audio recordings go to: www.shasti.org/instruction, then drop down the menu tab titled "Trigueirinho Instruction" and then click on "MP3 audios."

A Book to Be Written
A New Viewpoint of the Monad
Alopathic and Homeopathic Medicine
An Esoteric Dimension of Power
An Overview of Current Life
Angels and Humanity – 1
Angels and Humanity – 2
Angels and Humanity – 3
Angels and Humanity – 4
Bases of the Fiery World
Beyond Fire by Friction
Beyond Imperfection
Causal Body
Colors in Healing and the Formation of Our Light Vessel
Deep Healing
From the Human Kingdom to the Spiritual Kingdom
Getting through Today's Critical Times
Harmonization and Androgyny
How One Begins to Perceive One's Inner Self
How to Understand the Planetary Disasters
Human Trials | The Trials of the Soul
Information on the New Earth and the New Humanity
Inner and Outer Figueira
Instruction: a Step beyond Teaching
Liberating and Healing through Colors
Life in Cosmic Signs
New Supraterrestrial Pathways – 1
New Supraterrestrial Pathways – 2
New Supraterrestrial Pathways – 3
New Supraterrestrial Pathways – 4
Niskalkat
Noah's Vessel
On Vitality
Our Response to the Cosmos – 1
Our Response to the Cosmos – 2
Our Response to the Cosmos – 3
Our Response to the Cosmos – 4
Our Response to the Cosmos – 5
Our Response to the Cosmos – 6
Preparation for the Path of Initiation
Reflections on Illusion and Rescue
Reflections on Inner Attunement
Seeds of Inner Transformation
Seeking to Understand the Self

To Medical Doctors and Therapists
To Those Who Pray – 1
To Those Who Pray – 2
Towards Self Consecration
We are Part of the Cosmos
Working Spiritually with One's Mind
Working with the Feminine Polarity
Working with the Rays

www.ingramcontent.com/pod-product-compliance
Ingram Content Group UK Ltd.
Pitfield, Milton Keynes, MK11 3LW, UK
UKHW041641190726
13854UKWH00006B/2621

9 781948 430074